Fostering the Harvest

BUILDING REDEMPTIVE RELATIONSHIPS
TO EFFECTIVELY SHARE YOUR FAITH

AN EVANGELISM WORKSHOP FROM
BIBLICAL MINISTRIES WORLDWIDE

Fostering the Harvest

To order more copies of this book, visit www.amazon.com or call 866.216.1072.
To learn more about Biblical Ministries Worldwide, visit www.biblicalministries.org or call 770.339.3500.

ISBN 978-1475144307

Printed in the United States of America

Welcome

This workshop was designed by your friends at Biblical Ministries Worldwide for churches just like yours that are seeking to equip themselves for maximum ministry effectiveness and to reach the community all around them with the gospel of Jesus Christ. The facilitator should be the person most interested in evangelism in your church. The assumption is that he should "train saints to do the work of the ministry" (Ephesians 4:11-12). It is our prayer that this process will radically expand the outreach ministry of your congregation.

If there is some way in which we can improve these materials or serve you better, please feel free to contact us at

> Biblical Ministries Worldwide
> 1595 Herrington Road
> Lawrenceville, GA 30043
> 770.339.3500
> bmwhq@biblicalministries.org

Facilitators Guide

READ THIS FIRST!!! – You are vital to the success of this workshop. As the facilitator you have the potential to impact the evangelistic outreach of your church. It is recommended that you review each lesson before presenting it. The format for each session is four steps. Here are the simple steps to help you make this a success:

Step 1   Introduce the week's lesson. Beginning the second week, spend 5-8 minutes hearing reports of how people implemented the previous week's lesson.

Step 2   Play the approximately 25-40 minutes of teaching on the DVD. Dave Brown will cover the material one chapter at a time.

Step 3   Lead a discussion. After watching the DVD, take the time to discuss the questions provided at the end of the lesson, when available (note the boxes called "Discussion Time").

Step 4   Assist those in the group to make immediate application of the material. This fourth step is critical. Listening to the materials will be of no value unless there is practical and immediate application of the information. Your role is critical to facilitating application. During this step you should talk about what each one plans to do with this in the coming week.

SUPPLEMENTAL BOOKLET – *Shoe Leather* contains a series of extended lessons in the application of *Fostering the Harvest* principles. The sessions were delivered to a group of people who were given the assignment to implement *Fostering the Harvest* throughout their church. While some of the topics are directed primarily to these implementers, you may find the material in the other sessions of use as a follow-up workshop for those in your church that want to take the principles of *Fostering the Harvest* to the next level. We encourage the viewing of these sessions to see what part, if any, they might be of use in your ministry to reach the lost for Jesus Christ. (To order copies of *Shoe Leather*, visit www.amazon.com or call 866.216.1072.)

Table of Contents

A Reflection of My Devotion

How Believers Glorify God

When you boil down Christian ambition, our aim in life is to glorify God and enjoy Him. We do this in four basic ways: worshipping God, helping other believers become Christ-like through discipleship, sharing our faith, and living a holy life while fulfilling our calling (God-directed career path). Most all of what we do, think, and say that makes God happy falls under one of these four areas.

WORSHIP AND THANKSGIVING

Our Relationship With God

GOD'S GLORY

DISCIPLING BELIEVERS

Our Relationships With People

HOLINESS AND CALLING

EVANGELIZING UNBELIEVERS

> A heart and life that glorifies God is summed up in this – that we find our enjoyment in doing things solely for His enjoyment.

The areas of worship and holiness (the left side) are chiefly about our relationship with God. Evangelism and discipleship (the right side) are about our relationships with other people. For healthy believers, all four of these activities should take place in our personal lives on a regular basis.

Evangelism Glorifies God

As we have seen, part of glorifying God involves serving people. How does serving people glorify God? When you love an absolutely awesome person, you want to tell others about Him and give others the privilege of knowing Him. Maybe one day they could even become like Him!

We should all be driven by a passion to see more worshippers of Jesus Christ. As we tell others about Jesus Christ, we show Him that we truly believe He is worthy. As people commit their lives to Him, they too become reproducing worshippers. It's all about God.

> Evangelism springs from a heart of worship.
>
> Worship springs from a heart that has seen Jesus Christ change a life through evangelism.

DISCIPLESHIP

Evangelism — *Making Disciples Discipling to Christ*

Discipleship Proper — *Equipping Disciples Discipling in Christ*

Leadership Development — *Mentoring Leaders Discipling to Maturity*

Making and equipping disciples is our mission (Matthew 28:19-20), but beyond that, it should be our passion. Discipleship is an over-arching principle. It begins when you first meet an unbeliever; you disciple them to Christ. It continues after salvation as you get the new believer grounded in his or her faith, and it continues all the way to Christian maturity. Sharing Christ and making new disciples is the privilege of every one of Jesus' disciples, not just those who are gifted, and not just those who are in vocational ministry.[1]

> *"Go therefore and make disciples of all the nations, baptizing them in the name of the Father, and of the Son and of the Holy Spirit, teaching them to observe all things that I have commanded you. . . ."*
> Matthew 28:19-20

> Evangelism is a phase in the process of disciple-making.

---

[1] Someone in "vocational ministry" engages in ministry as a full-time job or career. This would normally include pastors, missionaries, evangelists, etc.

Barriers to Sharing My Faith

Most believers don't even think of reaching the lost one-by-one. It may be due to one or more problems that we face in Western culture.[2]

PRIORITY PROBLEM
(MY HEART'S LACK OF COMPASSION)

1. **DISTRACTION – "I'm just too busy; I have other competing priorities; I just don't have much of a heart for unsaved people."**
    We are too busy. Busyness and fatigue can be the main things that keep us from pursuing our relationship with God, and guarding His priorities in our lives. If we're honest, we'll recognize this as a heart issue. In the end we all do what we want to do.

2. **INTIMIDATION – "I would feel uneasy hanging around or talking with unbelievers. They drink and smoke and use foul words, and I don't appreciate that."**
    There is one thing that makes both believers and unbelievers uneasy – witnessing about Christ. The fear of man brings a snare. Perfect love casts out fear; love for Christ and His gospel and love for the lost can overcome your fear. Love of self makes us guard our comfort zone. Reach out; do it for Jesus' sake.

3. **DILUTION – "I just want to tell everyone that God is all about them. He wants to make them into all the wonderful things they can be."**
    In an effort to demonstrate "success" in numeric terms, some Christians compromise God's truth by watering down aspects of the gospel that are unpalatable to the unbeliever. Some present a gospel that is man-centered, offering a genie-of-the-lamp God who exists to help people achieve their dreams. But despite the use of similar terminology, this is "another gospel" rather than the true saving gospel of Christ (Galatians 1:6-9). "Another gospel" is the same gospel with the life-giving DNA changed.

PREPARATION PROBLEM
(MY HEAD'S LACK OF EDUCATION)

4. **INSTRUCTION (LACK OF) – "I've never learned a solid gospel presentation; I've never been trained to cultivate redemptive relationships; I don't know how to transition conversations. I won't be able to answer their questions."**
    Although many believers know the good news generally, they don't have their ideas in order with supporting Bible verses. They would struggle to present it well to someone else, and they don't know what to expect from unbelievers. There are books – even this workbook – and websites that can help you with this.

> The Ten-Minute Transformation –
> If God were to give us five minutes on the edge of hell followed by five minutes on the edge of heaven, we would never again have a problem with priorities.

> The medicine of the gospel has been prescribed by the Great Physician; we may neither dilute it nor add ingredients to make it more palatable; but we must serve it lovingly and understandingly.

---

[2] The term "Western culture" denotes the traditions, values, and way of life of people in Europe, America, and the lands of their former colonies.

PROXIMITY PROBLEM
(MY FEET'S WRONG DIRECTION)

5. **ISOLATION – "I've been taught for years not to befriend unbelievers. We Christians are hated by the world anyway; if I am Christ-like, they shouldn't like me."**

   In our zeal to stay unspotted from the world system, Christians are increasingly isolating themselves from those held captive by it. Churches are increasingly beset by a "cloister" mentality. Christians are failing to bring the gospel to the public in meaningful ways and seem to be waiting for the ungodly to come to them on Sunday mornings. While the world system and its proponents hate us, most unbelievers do not hate Christians. In various cultures, they can be very curious about and open to the truth of the gospel.

6. **INSTITUTION – "I really don't have the time because we're too busy with ministry at church; I'm waiting for the church to organize something."**

   Over-scheduling can be a problem, with larger churches in particular. Gifted and talented people get involved in multiple in-house ministries serving believers and spend most weeknights and weekends at the church building. They simply have no time to mingle with unbelievers.

   If sharing Christ is the privilege and duty of each believer, we are not privileged to ignore Christ's command because the organized church is not helping us. On the other hand, if we have not been equipped to share our faith, we will be afraid to do so. The more afraid and insecure we are, the more we want to operate as a group (the wolf pack mentality). If we move as a group, we can go out on visitation teams, or we can invite unbelievers to come into our church buildings for an event. In both situations, we are being evangelists by proxy, not in person.

DISCUSSION TIME!

1. Being brutally honest, does our weakness in sharing our faith lie primarily with our priorities, our preparation, or our proximity? What about you personally?

2. If you haven't been equipped so that you can capably share your faith, what might your heart do when it is touched by the need to reach unbelievers?

3. Do you think the culture in your church encourages isolation and ministry only at the church campus? What could be done to bring a better balance?

Four Principles from Antioch

In Acts 11:19-33, we have a description of an awesome church that was planted without a human plan, and without pastors or missionary church-planters! It was the #1 church-planting church of the New Testament.

The Organic Principle

The first principle we can learn from Antioch (Acts 11:19-21) is that a local church is first **organic** and then **organizational.**

ORGANIC – By "*organic*" we mean that a local body of believers is a living thing (like a garden or orchard). In 1 Corinthians 3:5-9, Paul wrote to the Corinthian church, "You are God's agricultural project." Birth, growth, maturity, reproduction, and death are all principles of life. The laws of life apply to a local church and its members. On average, local churches have about 70 people, and the average lifespan of churches is about 70 years, the same lifespan as a human being (this is known as the 70/70 Principle).

Attract sheep from other folds or give birth to new sheep?

One rule of life is that healthy living things reproduce after their kind. For instance,

- Healthy sheep reproduce _____
- Healthy believers reproduce _____
- Healthy leaders reproduce _____
- Healthy churches reproduce _____

The Antioch church had life! It was started through a massive effort by **transformed and enthusiastic** believers. The evangelism was **non-professional and non-institutional.** There is no evidence that there were church-planters or pastors; there was no structure or programs. Jewish believers had moved into the city and were using their new network of relationships in the neighborhood to share Christ with Jews. Some traveled through Antioch on business trips and used their network of relationships in the marketplace to share Christ with Greeks.

Is your church healthy? How "spiritually reproductive" would your church be without programs or professionals? Church statisticians have found that the organic life of churches in America is in peril: 85% of churches are stagnant or dying; most churches are struggling to maintain buildings built by previous generations; about 85% of churches report no conversions in the previous year; 60 churches are closing and 12 new ones are opening each week in America.

ORGANIZATIONAL – By "*organizational*" we mean that the Church benefits from structure (like a tomato cage guides the plant's growth). Barnabas was sent to Antioch by the Jerusalem church to help guide the group's growth (Acts 11:22-26). In 1 Corinthians 3:9-14, Paul said, "You are God's building project." Building projects have a design, builders, a cornerstone, and other materials that form a structure.

Having a tomato cage doesn't mean you have a healthy tomato plant. Ideally, your church should only create an "evangelism program" when believers are witnessing wildly and could use a little guidance! In Antioch, so many people trusted Christ, that the Jerusalem church sent out Barnabas to encourage and organize things a bit.

As a church grows over time, "institutionalism" almost invariably sets in. Although a pastor's success is often gauged by the size and design of his "tomato cage," most pastors stay focused on the spiritual health of the congregation and are grieved when they see the fire dying in the heart of the church. A local church's health is an average of the health of each believer in the congregation.

The One-by-One Principle

Acts 11:19-21 also demonstrates that the Antioch believers shared their faith as individuals rather than waiting for an institution to organize something. The Great Commission was given to every disciple. Although 1 Corinthians 14:23-24 mentions that unbelievers might be present in a gathering of believers and hear the gospel, the New Testament norm was that most evangelism was done by "the church disbursed" rather than by "the church gathered."

Do we have a good balance in our American churches? If you were to brainstorm how you intend to reach your community with the gospel, you would typically get answers like special evangelistic meetings, a sportsmen's banquet, a cantata, evangelistic teams, a coffee shop, a float in the parade, etc. Very seldom will anyone raise his or her hand and say, "Let's build relationships with our neighbors and coworkers and win them to Christ one-by-one."

Evangelism is not primarily the duty of the organized church; it is the duty of the individual believer. A pastor shares his faith, not because he is a pastor or a pro at sharing the gospel, but because he is a Christian. Church leaders are given by God to equip believers to evangelize (Ephesians 4:11-12). They may organize believers to do evangelism together, but believers are not to sit back and wait for the church to do something.

The "Go" Principle

Matthew 28:19-20 lays out the Great Commission. In it Jesus used the word **"go"** and not the word **"come."** Sharing your faith is not merely, "Y'all come and hear the preacher." The believers in Antioch (Acts 11:19-21) had no church building and no special services or speakers to which they could invite people. They went out with fire in their hearts, found unbelievers, and enthusiastically shared Christ with them.

**Bring Them To
"Fortress Functions"**
(Find, Bring, Win)

Unbelievers

**Believers Say
"You Come"**

Church Property

Historically, we have focused on bringing unbelievers into "the fortress" to sit through our functions and hear the gospel. The "seeker friendly" debate involved how much we should change our church culture to accommodate unbelievers. But it seems that both traditional and market-driven churches have made a sad presupposition: "believers simply don't share their faith, so unbelievers will only hear the gospel if they come to church."

**Go As
"The Field Force"**
(Find, Win, Bring)

Church Property

**Believers Say
"Let's Go"**

Unbelievers

Hopefully, we can help you shift your evangelism paradigm from "find, bring, win" to "find, win, bring."

In general, people often become Christians because of relational influence rather than by attendance at events.

Led to Christ through a trusting relationship - 77%
- *Family member 48%*
- *Friend 29%*

Led to Christ during a group event - 23%
- *Youth event 4%*
- *Sermon at a church or S.S. class 14%*
- *Evangelistic event 4%*
- *Radio, television 1%*

Barna Research 1995

"Too many believers are evangelists by proxy but not in person."
Vance Havner

SURROUNDING GOD

Imagine putting God in a box! Yet, in many circles, that is exactly what local churches have done. "God lives inside the walls of our church building; come and find Him here." We have surrounded God with our culture and said that unbelievers have to muster the courage to come into our buildings, wear our clothes, and know our liturgy in order to find God.

Different styles seem to flourish in turn as culture changes. Starting in the revival era of the 1880s and 90s, the Church in the cultural West shifted strongly to institutional evangelism done by ministry professionals. But over the past 25 years, culture has been swinging away from institutions; people have become increasingly cynical about churches being "full of hypocrites" and "always out for your money."

People in our fast-paced, impersonal, institutional, relationally dysfunctional Western society are hungry for truth, but they are very skeptical of the thing called "church." Many want to know about God and the Bible, but they don't like church. For this reason, the proclamational and invitational approaches to evangelism don't seem to be working very well, and cults have damaged the confrontational style.

If we can learn to personally communicate God's truth to unbelievers one-by-one in the context of our everyday lives and relationships, many more people may come to faith in Christ. For this reason, "evangelistically healthy" churches in the next couple of decades will be those that have equipped their people to share the gospel personally in addition to the traditional methods used by local churches.

What We Have Been Doing — Church / GOD / Culture — Unbelievers — What We Need to Do — Church / GOD / Culture — Personal Relationships

The Conversion Growth Principle

Want to test your church's evangelistic health to see whether you are making new disciples of Christ? Ask for a show of hands in answer to two questions on a Sunday morning:
- "How many of you were led to Christ by someone in this congregation?"
- "How many of you have been a believer less than five years?"

See Appendix A for charts about various evangelistic styles and methods

In most evangelical churches, 5-7% of the congregation is "conversion growth;" they were led to saving faith by someone in the congregation or at a church meeting. And, on average, less than half of that number has been in Christ less than five years. The Antioch church was perhaps 90% conversion growth!

What again is the organic principle? Life begets life. We add sheep to the sheepfold by giving birth to new sheep. Some churches grow by getting a better grain-dispenser, adding molasses to their grain, or getting new stone walls for the fold! Why not purpose in your hearts to become a biblically healthy church where there are many lambs among the sheep.

Learning the Substance of the Gospel

Having a presentation of the gospel "down cold" will arm you with the truth and with phenomenal confidence! If you don't like the presentation below, develop your own![3]

The Bad News - Headed for a Bad Place

1. **God is HOLY and PERFECT, and He requires each of us, made in His image, to be PERFECT.**
   - **1 Peter 1:15-16** – we must be HOLY.
   - **James 2:10** – God says that even ONE sin breaks the whole law.
     > Illustration #1: God's law is like a chain of commands. How many links in a chain have to break before a beautiful chandelier falls from the ceiling? Breaking one of God's commands breaks the chain of fellowship.
   - **Matthew 5:48** – we must be PERFECT.
     > Illustration #2: When it comes to food, we utterly reject poison. How much gasoline would you like in your milk? Half and half? A teaspoon? An eyedropper? God wants perfection.

2. **God calls breaking His law "SIN" and says that ALL of us have sinned.**
   - **1 John 1:8, 10** – We're DECEIVING ourselves if we say we haven't sinned.
   - **Romans 3:23** - ALL have sinned and fall short of what God requires.
     > Illustration #3: I'm a pretty good guy; let's say I've only committed three sins a day – one sinful thought, one sinful word, and one sinful action. But in one year, that's over 1,000 sins; then multiply that by the years of my life. Whew! That's a lot of sins!

3. **God says that the just and proper penalty for sin is DEATH.**
   - **Romans 6:23** – the payment for sin is DEATH. Death in the Bible starts with separation from fellowship with God in this life.
     > Illustration #4: When the phone line is cut, we say "the phone is dead." Why? It is cut off from communication with the outside world. A computer without a modem may function well, but it cannot communicate with the outside world. Our spirit has been cut off from communication with God because of our sin (see also Ephesians 2:1).
   - **Revelation 20:11-15** – One day, God will execute JUDGMENT against sinners; afterward, there is separation from God forever in a place called THE LAKE OF FIRE.

4. **I cannot SAVE myself from judgment by GOOD or RELIGIOUS works.**
   - **Titus 3:5** – we are not saved by WORKS OF RIGHTEOUSNESS.
     > Illustration #5: Let's say my wallet is a record book of my sins (take out your wallet). I can really turn my life around (turn it), or turn over a whole new leaf (flip it), or fill my life with good works (cover it). But look, the record book is still there. All of my years of lawful driving won't erase my speeding offence.
   - **Ephesians 2:8-9** – salvation is not by WORKS; rather, it is God's FREE GIFT.
     > Illustration #6: Imagine how insulted you would be if you gave me a gift, and I started whipping out $20 bills to pay for it. How much do I have to pay you to change the gift to a bargain purchase? (1 cent)
   - **Isaiah 64:6** – God considers our good works as FILTHY RAGS.
     > Illustration #7: Who was Jesus toughest on? The Pharisees, the leaders of God's own Jewish religion, men who were known for their good and religious works!

"God had only one Son, and He made Him an evangelist."
R. C. Lucas

POTENCY WARNING
The information on these two pages contains life-giving seed. It can change a person from spiritually dead to alive, from blind to seeing, from deaf to hearing, from hell-bound to heaven-bound, from alien to adopted child of God.

Change the DNA in the seed and it will lose its life-giving power.

"All true theology has an evangelistic thrust, and all true evangelism is theology in action."
J. I. Packer

---

[3] This presentation borrows some ideas from the excellent Evangelism Explosion materials. You may wish to purchase their training program. Find out more at www.eeinternational.org.

The Good News - He Took My Place

5. **God LOVES you and me, and He made a PLAN for us to be REUNITED with Him and SAVED from the coming judgment.**
   - John 3:16 – Because God loved us, He sent His SON.

6. **Jesus died as a SUBSTITUTE for us. He paid the PENALTY for our sin. By this Jesus defeated SIN, DEATH, SATAN and HELL – and He ROSE AGAIN!**
   - Romans 5:8 – Christ died FOR US.
   - 2 Corinthians 5:20-21 – God takes our SIN and places it on Jesus, and He takes Jesus' RIGHTEOUSNESS and places it on US.
     > Illustration #8: During the Great Depression, a young man was brought in before a judge in Chicago for stealing fruit. The young man said he was starving. The judge found him guilty as charged and was told that the fine was $10. The judge then paid the fine and commented that the community should be helping its needy. Did the judge uphold justice? What if he had dismissed the charges due to the young man's poverty?

7. **God offers each of us the FREE GIFT of eternal life ONLY through Jesus' death.**
   - Acts 4:12 – There is NO other way.
   - John 14:6 – Jesus is THE way, THE truth, and THE life (not merely A way).
     > Illustration #9: Many people say that Christians are bigoted to believe that Jesus is the only way. Let's say a ship like the Titanic was sinking, and God sent along a boat to save the drowning. Imagine someone treading water saying, "What, just one ship? Do you think your ship is the only ship?"

8. **To receive God's gift of forgiveness of sins . . .**
   - Acts 3:19 – Change your mind about trusting in anything but Christ for eternal life
   - Romans 10:9-10 – Trust God to forgive your sin based on His death, burial, and resurrection
   - John 1:12 – RECEIVE God's free gift through His Son.
     > Illustration #10: Suppose I gave you a million-dollar check and had enough money in the bank to cover it. You could take the check, jump up and down waving it and telling all your friends that you are rich . . . but you're not truly rich until you do what? You must do business with God – cash or deposit the check.

> See Appendix B for tips on the Security of the Believer

Being Able to Say It Quickly

A man is awake and alert but has 30 seconds to live. Clearly communicate the gospel to him!

1. **God is HOLY and PERFECT and He requires each of us, made in His image, to be PERFECT.**
2. **God calls breaking His law "SIN" and says that ALL of us have sinned.**
3. **God says that the just and proper penalty for sin is DEATH.**
4. **I cannot SAVE myself from judgment by GOOD or RELIGIOUS works.**
5. **God LOVES us; He made a PLAN for us to be REUNITED with Him and be SAVED from the coming judgment.**
6. **Jesus died as a SUBSTITUTE for us. He paid the PENALTY for our sin. By this Jesus defeated SIN, DEATH, SATAN and HELL – and He rose again!**
7. **God offers each of us the FREE GIFT of eternal life ONLY through Jesus' death.**
8. **To receive God's gift of forgiveness of sins, turn from your self-rule, believe what God has done for you through Jesus Christ, and receive His gift of forgiveness.**

The Starting Point of the Gospel

QUESTION: Where do you start when the time is right to present someone with the good news?

ANSWER: It depends on where they are.

For instance, you meet a guy and start in with, "God loves you and has a wonderful plan for your life." But if the person is a European, he may respond, "So you believe God is a specific person and lives in a specific place? Interesting. God is many things to many people. I believe God is a force flowing through both of us." OK, you'll have to back up.

What happened? You presumed that he is your average 1960s American monotheist who presupposes certain things are true, just like you do: there is a single God, living in a place called heaven, who has revealed Himself and His will in the Bible. You presumed that he is merely confused about how to get to heaven.

Evangelistic training courses virtually all suffer from a "canned approach." Learning a gospel presentation well is a huge step, but the farther a culture is from a biblical worldview, the more you will have to learn about apologetics and other philosophies and religions. American culture is rapidly taking on a global flavor, so you'll need to develop your approach further.

See Appendix C for sample apologetics arguments and resources

PRACTICE TIME!

Review these last two pages, then break up into groups of two or three and test each other.

First, try to get the eight points down clearly – four points of bad news; four points of good news.

If you will meet again as a group, learn the verses and illustrations and test each other.

Be kind!

The Gospel — *Growing Understanding and Faith*

We can receive God's gift by repentance and faith.
Jesus, God in human flesh, died as a substitute for me.
God loves us and made a plan for our salvation.

I cannot save myself through good/religious works.
Death is separation from God now and in hell.
God's law says the proper penalty for sin is death.
Man has broken God's law and is a sinner.
God and His law are holy; God requires man to be holy.
MOVING INTO THE GOSPEL

Apologetics

Jesus is God.
God's special revelation of Himself is the Bible.
God exists.
PRESUPPOSITIONAL BASE

In the World, But Not of the World

There are several things to note about the little patch of land known as an unbeliever's life:

- It is not located right next to you (though the person may live next door).
- It has soil that may need some cultivation.
- It has some thickets growing in it that are harmful to him and to you.

The World of Unbelievers or Unbelievers in the World

"Love not the world. . . ." 1 John 2:15
"For God so loved the world. . . ." John 3:16

There's a seeming contradiction in these two verses! These words were written by the same author using the same Greek word for "world" and the same word for "love." How can we reconcile the seeming contradiction? The term "world" can refer to either "the world of unbelievers" or "unbelievers in the world."

- ### The World of Unbelievers (Anti-God Leaders)
  This is a system of ideas, people, and institutions that is hostile toward God and His Son (John 15:18-19). In his first epistle John said that the world system pushes three values – pursuing possessions, pleasures, and positions (1 John 2:15-17). Paul said in 2 Corinthians 6:17 that we are to **separate from the proponents of the world system and never be yoked together with them.**

  The media, movie industry, and public educational systems are probably the leading proponents of the world of unbelievers. Some of your coworkers and neighbors may even be proponents of the world system; they are openly hostile to God and His people. Many Christians (maybe you!) have taken heat from these people at work or in the marketplace of ideas. These people will not normally allow you to be their friend. Showing resolute kindness and selfless love to these people over time is perhaps the best way of piercing their hard hearts; normally you will not win them through cunning apologetic arguments or confrontational challenges.

- ### Unbelievers in the World (Pro-Self Followers)
  These are people born into and held captive by the world system (2 Timothy 2:24-26). They are spiritually dead, blind, and deaf and will not seek after God until God begins drawing them to Himself. Paul mentioned in 1 Corinthians 5:9-11 that Christians are **not to separate** from unbelievers. In 1 Corinthians 9:19-23, he adds that we are to **get next to unbelievers for the gospel's sake.**

  Most of your neighbors and the people at work are merely unbelievers in the world. They believe what they've been told by their unbelieving parents, teachers, friends, and the media. When they rejected creationism, they didn't do it for intellectual reasons – teachers taught them about evolution and nothing else, their friends agreed, and their mind was made up. Their sentiments are not openly anti-God as much as they are simply "pro-self."

  You can often build friendships with these people because God has used the limited truth they have received to build their curiosity to know more about God, the Bible, and Jesus in a non-threatening, informal way where they can have their questions answered.

Unbelievers in the World

World of Unbelievers

While the world system hates us, our unsaved acquaintances should think well of us. The early church was well thought of by the Jerusalem community (Acts 2) and elders/ pastors are to have a good reputation with unbelievers (1 Timothy 3).

A Caution about Who Is Influencing Whom

Some believers, weak in their spiritual devotion, self-discipline, or personal identity, are susceptible to worldly peer pressure and run into trouble when they hang around people held captive by the world system. This is particularly true of Christian teens. For this reason, many parents and church leaders tell teens not to have unsaved friends.

However, there must come a time when believers stand to their spiritual feet, put peer-dependency behind them, and identify with Christ while in the world. Personal discipleship and accountability help believers arrive at this point much more quickly.

We must periodically ask ourselves two questions in relational evangelism: **Where are my feet? Where is my heart?**

Not in the World
(Spends Non-Work Time with Believers)

FRUSTRATED Not in the World Of the World	ISOLATED Not in the World Not of the World
Of The World *(Worldly Heart)*	*Not of the World* *(Spiritual Heart)*
DEFEATED In the World Of the World	INSULATED In the World Not of the World

In the World
(Spends Non-Work Time with Unbelievers)

1 Corinthians 5:9-10 – Keep company with unbelievers, although they are sinners
1 Corinthians 9:19-27 – Become like them, yet not in a sinful, lawless way; be self-disciplined
2 Corinthians 6:14-18 – We don't have yoking, fellowship, accord, or deep relations with them
1 Peter 4:3-4 – It is natural for them to be perturbed at you because you don't party, etc.

Being Misunderstood by Christians

It is a natural tendency for believers to cloister themselves from a wicked society. The Jewish leaders of Jesus' day advocated separation from those who were noted for sin:
- They confused "in the world" with "of the world."
- They hated sin and sinners.
- They cloistered themselves.
- They used intimidation to bring conformity.

Jesus, who was perfect and holy, understood that hanging around sinners did not make you unholy; in fact, He said, it is the sick that need a doctor, not those who are well. Jesus knowingly discipled an unbeliever named Judas for three years and called him "friend."

Other believers may misunderstand you if you hang around unbelievers. Jesus had that problem and was thus accused of being a drunkard and a friend of prostitutes, criminals, and those known for their sinfulness (Matthew 9:11 and 11:19). Welcome to the fellowship of Jesus' sufferings; be ready to face the Pharisee mindset.

FIREMEN & FIRE

To rescue people from a burning building, firemen must go inside, but they do not go in unprotected; they wear material that insulates them from the flames.

They are insulated, but not isolated.

BOATS & WATER

The boat must be in the water, but there must be no water in the boat.

"And have compassion on some who are wavering; save others by snatching them out of the fire, hating even the tunic defiled by their bodies."
Jude 22-23 NRSV

JESUS & MANKIND

God could have saved us from above. "Relating" was illustrated in the incarnation. Jesus became fully one of us . . . yet without sin.

Similarly, our evangelistic potency is increased if we are "incarnational" in our approach.

A Caution about the Dark Side

Look at the diagram below. My neighbor and I have professional lives and personal lives. Our professional worlds don't overlap because we don't work together. Our personal lives don't touch in a meaningful way except to comment on the weather or the condition of the roads. Although the gospel message has transformed my whole life, the *gospel message* is part of my personal life. My neighbor's personal world often contains a dark side where they engage in sinful behaviors either privately or publicly.

MY LIFE   **MY NEIGHBOR'S LIFE**

The Wall of Unfamiliarity and Different Priorities

To communicate the gospel most effectively, I need to bring our two **personal lives together** so that the gospel can touch their personal life. The caution, of course, is that I not allow myself to be tainted by their dark side. Some people have a very big dark side! I must get next to them while remaining consecrated to the Lord (1 Corinthians 9:21).

So, what are the sinful behaviors of a person's "dark side"? And how can we spend time with unbelievers and not take part in their sin? No doubt, Jesus and his disciples beheld some bothersome things while sitting with tax-collectors, harlots, and other sinners. Yet Jesus remained pure.

How you flesh this out will vary from family to family and church to church. You need to search the Scriptures, pray to have the mind of the Spirit, think through these issues, and talk them over with your family and other families in the church who are reaching out to the lost.

DISCUSSION TIME!

Beyond simple answers, discuss why and whether your response might change with certain parameters added:

- Will you go to the block party or the July 4ᵗʰ cook-out if alcohol is present?
- What would you do if you invited Bob and Launa to your home for a cook-out and they brought beer?
- What if Steve and Kim invite you over to watch a movie, and you find it's a little too immodest and profane?
- What if Jim has very immodest posters on the wall of his garage and wants you to help him work on his car?
- What if Mitch calls you in tears from Gillie's Pub and wants you to come over and talk?
- Would you let your son attend Isaac and Sheila's son's bar mitzvah? Attend Mass with the O'Malley family on Friday night?

See Appendix D for helpful tips on making decisions as a Christian on these thorny issues.

The Sower and the Fields

There are two things on this earth that will last forever: the Word of God and the souls of people. It is our privilege as believers to bring the one to the other. We all need to bring the good news of Jesus Christ to the people at work, in our neighborhood, in the stores where we shop, and in our communities.

Walk in wisdom toward those who are outside, redeeming the time.
Colossians 4:5

We are trying to bring unchanging truth to changing people in a myriad of changing cultures in a changing world with an increasing rate of change. As co-laborers with God in the harvest, we must know the seed well, but we must also be students of the field. We must understand our **times**, understand our **culture,** and understand our **contacts** within that culture. We also need to understand **ourselves**.

Understanding Your Times

Local, national, and international events will take place that profoundly impact the thinking, feelings, and outlook of people around you. **As a general rule change opens people to more change.** The gospel is a form of change. A society in upheaval is more open to the gospel.

Immediately after the World Trade Center towers fell in New York City, there was a temporary openness of people to talk about spiritual and meaningful things. Citizens of the Soviet block countries have shown interest in the gospel since the Berlin Wall fell. The end of apartheid, massive cultural change, and increased crime in South Africa have opened many to the gospel. You must stay informed and seize (buy up, redeem) the opportunities to present the gospel when change is in the air.

"There were in Israel men of Issachar, who understood the times and knew what Israel should do."
1 Chronicles 12:32

Understanding Your Culture

Some of you have lived in your community your whole life. Though you know your culture intuitively, you may have never stopped to think about it or analyze it. Others of you may have moved into your area recently; you're learning the culture, but it takes some time. A Georgian is different from a New Englander who is different from a Texan who is different from a Californian.

EXERCISE 1: Get in a group and take a few minutes to circle which words or phrases are indicative of your area:

Reserved	Outgoing	Mobile	Immobile
Value the old	Value the new	Polite	Rude
Loud	Quiet	Closed to new ideas	Open to new ideas
Up front	Behind your back	Serious	Humorous
Laid back	Intense	Surface chats	Deep talks
Sincere	Sarcastic	Quick friendships	Slow friendships
Traditional	Unconventional	Churched	Unchurched
Blue collar	White collar	Western religions	Eastern religions
Costly entertainment	Cheap entertainment	Country music	Rock music
Fine dining	Fast food	Suits at work	Jeans at work
New vehicles abound	Old vehicles abound	40-hour workweek	60-hour workweek
Kentucky Derby	NASCAR	Value change	Dislike change
Impulsive	Reflective	Mom at home	Mom in marketplace
Double-income-no-kids	Families	Dad below 40	Dad above 40
Lots of friends	A few good friends	Urban/suburban	Rural

"We cannot evangelize unless we understand the Word and the world."
Donald MacLeod

Decades ago, our culture was fairly homogenous; although people had different ethnic backgrounds, as a society we were very similar. That is changing; today our culture is far more diverse and fragmented. Many ethnic groups are cloistering to preserve their culture. In a few more years, America may be the largest Spanish-speaking nation on earth; Latinos are now the leading minority.

Therefore, understanding your culture may be almost impossible, except to say that it is changing rapidly and is very diverse. In such cultures, some churches are being started to embrace diversity with names like "Victory World Church" or "Freedom International Church." Multi-culturalism is actually the selling point of the church.

Winning people to Christ relationally in such a culture can be tricky. You must take the time to learn the cultural background of each person and family through casual conversations in which you ask many questions. One huge benefit is that often immigrants feel ostracized by the general public and respond to someone reaching out to them with love and a desire to understand.

> *"Behold, I say to you, lift up your eyes and look at the fields for they are already white for harvest! And he who reaps receives wages, and gathers fruit for eternal life, that both he who sows and he who reaps may rejoice together."*
> *John 4:35-36*

Understanding Your Contacts

Everyone is at a different stage and speed in his or her spiritual journey. Although there are no spiritual categories in reality (other than Christian and non-Christian), we've provided a chart below to understand how people typically progress spiritually.

EXERCISE 2: Study the chart from the bottom upward. Where are you on the chart? Where is your neighbor? Your co-worker?

THE SPIRITUAL JOURNEY	
Setting vision for future ministry	+10
Experiencing effective ministry to groups of believers	+9
Developing leadership skills	+8
Growing in commitment of time, talents and treasures	+7
Recognizing and utilizing spiritual gifts	+6
Understanding Bible doctrines and sharing the faith	+5
Growing in Bible study and the spiritual disciplines	+4
Learning basic doctrine and seeing behavioral changes	+3
Adopting a Christian identity	+2
Getting assurance of salvation	+1
New Christian	0
Seeking forgiveness by faith	-1
Giving in to the gospel and repenting of self-rule	-2
Recognizing a personal problem in relation to God	-3
Wrestling with questions about God, Bible, and the gospel	-4
Grasping the implications of the gospel	-5
Comprehension of the basic gospel	-6
Developing a positive attitude toward the Bible and God	-7
Questioning existing religious concept of God	-8
Has a religious awareness but no knowledge of God	-9
Has no conscious awareness of a Supreme Being	-10

SELFLESS SERVANT

SPIRITUAL GROWTH

SELFISH SINNER

> Where are you in your spiritual journey?

Understanding Yourselves

Sometimes, it is not the gospel that is the difficulty, nor is it our neighbors; it is just us. Some of us are just not wired as relational people. Others of us seem to be gifted as "people-persons" who have never met a stranger. We will earn the overcomer's crown when we evangelize. **All of us** are responsible to go out there, share the gospel, and make disciples; but giftedness helps some do it more easily.

There are many ways to study people from an observational standpoint. The Greek philosopher Hippocrates came up with **four temperaments**; they were popularized for believers in Tim LaHaye's Spirit Controlled Temperaments. The four temperaments have been further analyzed in the Solving the People Puzzle seminar by Walk Thru the Bible.

EXERCISE 3: Take a few minutes and have some fun discerning your temperament. How might your temperament affect your ability to share your faith and minister to others?

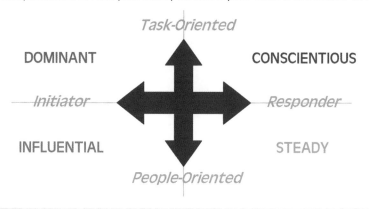

	DOMINANT (Choleric)	INFLUENTIAL (Sanguine)	STEADY (Phlegmatic)	CONSCIENTIOUS (Melancholic)
MOTTO	Get it done now	Get everyone on board	Get along with others	Get it done right
STRENGTHS	Confident Determined Independent Decisive Goal-oriented Accepts challenge	Persuasive Outgoing Enthusiastic Articulate Humorous Optimistic	Supportive Dependable/reliable Efficient/Practical Diplomatic Loyal Good listener	Orderly/thorough Self-disciplined Analytical Idealistic Diplomatic Creative
WEAKNESSES	Impatient Threatened Domineering Insensitive Self-sufficient Overlooks risks	Undisciplined Restless Lacks follow-through Braggart Exaggerates Manipulative	Stingy Indecisive Spectator Lacks initiative Stubborn Procrastinates	Perfectionist Self-centered Moody Impractical Critical Too cautious
BIBLE LEADER	Paul	Peter	Abraham	Moses
ORIENTATION	Task-initiator	People-initiator	People-responder	Task-responder
EVANGELISTIC PREFERENCES	Prefers the proclamational or confrontational styles	Prefers relational basis, and moves conversations easily and naturally to the gospel	Prefers long-term, relationship before moving slowly into spiritual topics and the gospel	Prefers a thorough explanation of the gospel - to a person or group.

* Virtually everyone is a combination of two or more temperaments
** Good moral training and self-discipline helps to suppress the weaknesses and release the strengths
*** These are for self-evaluation, not to label others and doom them to failure!

> Giftedness in evangelism affects our ability to respond but not our responsibility!

> **EXERCISE TIME!**
>
> Analyze your culture using Exercise 1; discuss how your culture might make sharing the gospel difficult or easy.
>
> Using Exercise 2, have you had enough meaningful conversations with neighbors and co-workers to know where they are spiritually?
>
> Using Exercise 3, can you tell why building relationships might be difficult or easy for you? Is your spouse different? How might personality affect someone's evangelistic style?

The Gulf and the Bridge

We have a challenge. Those fields we've been discussing aren't just a step away. Though an unbeliever's property may border yours, they may be far away from a relational standpoint. We must get across a gulf to reach the fields where we'll sow the seed.

The Gulf of Unfamiliarity

Between you and most of the unbelievers around you is the "gulf of unfamiliarity." You have no relationship with them. You would feel a little worried if a stranger came up to you and said, "I love you; here is a gift." You would feel even more awkward if he wound up and lobbed the gift to you from the far cliff.

Church "Fortress"   **World System**

Gulf of Unfamiliarity

> All evangelism is relational; you have a good relationship, a poor relationship, or no relationship.

To give an unbeliever the gift of the gospel in a personal way, you need to do three things: **1) build a truss system, 2) lay the planks, and then 3) cross the bridge you have built.** Crossing is risky without the trusses and planks firmly in place.

The Truss System of a Credible Lifestyle

The truss system is your lifestyle, your ethical integrity, your kindness, thoughtfulness, selflessness, your personal potency, and your credibility.

At work, if you are known for "fudging the numbers," stealing store supplies, cheating on your hours, or telling dirty jokes, don't even try to throw relational planks on your truss. People don't want to hear what you have to say. **People judge the credibility of the message by the credibility of the messenger.** They have judged Jesus as "unfit" in light of your life. They don't want what you have.

Followers of Jesus Christ must be highly contagious people. We have to live a life worth imitating, have a joy worth coveting, have a purpose worth seeking, and have a relationship with God that sparks amazement and curiosity. Without saying a word, unbelievers can be drawn to Christ by our way of living.

> At the restaurant, don't leave a tract but not a tip.

> *KEEP CLEAN!*
> *" . . . Keep your behavior excellent among the Gentiles, so that in the thing in which they slander you as evildoers, they may on account of your good deeds, as they observe them, glorify God in the day of visitation [on the day God visits them with salvation]."*
> *1 Peter 2:12*

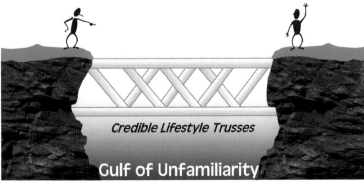

Credible Lifestyle Trusses

Gulf of Unfamiliarity

As a Christian, the core values, work ethic, and worldview that I hold in my personal life should overflow into my life in my neighborhood and in the marketplace. This distinctive difference should arouse curiosity in others about my personal life. What makes me tick? Why am I refreshingly different from others? Will this curiosity be a sufficient relational bridge to share the gospel? Normally not.

Our way of life will not save unbelievers; it will merely create thirst in them for whatever makes us different. Lifestyle is not evangelism. The term "lifestyle evangelism" used by Joe Aldrich was meant to stress this first of three stages in reaching out to unbelievers.

The Planks of Relationship

Once an unbeliever knows about your credibility, you can begin to add relational planks to the bridge. Often you are laying the planks at the same time you are building the truss system. Every word or act of kindness or service lays a new plank on the bridge. Every word or act of selfishness, even our mistakes, tears up or damages those planks.

TALK MUST FOLLOW WALK
Warning! Our relationships with unbelievers won't save them; they will merely create a thirst for whatever makes us different. Charitable deeds in helping the poor, the oppressed, and the needy are not the gospel. They are relational planks that can pave the bridge for the messenger. Compare Jesus' ministry with the "social gospel" of churches and Christian organizations in the 19th and 20th centuries. Jesus' healing, feeding, and helping unbelievers were accompanied by His teaching about the gospel of the kingdom. The social gospel alleviated disease, famine, and human suffering but had no gospel truth connected with it. Unbelievers were made healthier and happier with no remedy for a Christless eternity.

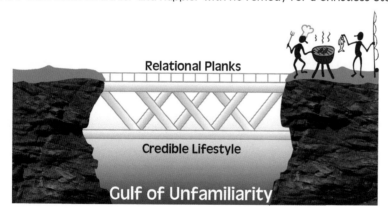

LAYING DOWN PLANKS
Giving a coworker a ride to work, taking care of the neighbors' dog while they're away, having the little league team over for a cook-out, weeding a garden bed for a sick friend, throwing a baby shower for an unwed mother, having a conversation with the deli worker, getting extra ballgame tickets for the guys at the garage, playing hoops with the guys at the college, chatting with a neighbor over the back fence – these are a few ways to build relationships with unbelievers all around you.

TEARING UP PLANKS
Similarly, there are thousands of ways to tear up the planks such as blowing leaves or lawn clippings onto their property, having children who are unkind or unruly, having a pit bull or other dog that doesn't help with relational coziness, being irritatingly friendly or competing with them for recognition or promotion at work or in a community organization. Be careful! There are Christians who, for the sake of protecting their fence line or bushes, have forever lost the opportunity to share Christ with their neighbors!

The Three Musketeers of Effective Ministry (Romans 12:11)

- **Ethos** – Ethical integrity
- **Pathos** – A passion for God and people
- **Logos** – A thorough knowledge of the Word of God

(And don't forget Dartagnian the lover)
Philos – Loving kindness toward others (Rom. 12:10)

"If sinners will be damned, at least let them leap into hell over our bodies."
C.H. Spurgeon

The Gulf Span

There is a danger in taking too long to build your bridge, and many Christians are very passive bridge-builders. How long might this bridge-building take? It depends upon **your times, your culture and your contacts** (as mentioned above).

If your times, your culture or your contacts' lives are in upheaval, the cliffs move closer together, and you could possibly build a bridge in one conversation. These are what missionaries call **"reaping fields."** Jesus mentioned Samaria as a field "white unto harvest" in John 4:35. A few years later, in Acts 8:5-8, Philip saw multitudes come to saving faith in Christ in Samaria.

If the times are stable, the culture is materialistic and cynical, and your contact's life is smooth, the cliffs are often far apart. In such circumstances, it may take you many years to build such a long bridge. These are what missionaries call **"sowing fields."**

REAPING FIELDS – SHORT BRIDGES
- Samaria
- Post 1989 Russia
- Post 9/11 America

SOWING FIELDS – LONG BRIDGES
- Post-modern Europe
- New England
- Pacific Northwest

You may be thinking of your neighbor right now and grumbling, "That's going to be one long bridge!" Don't despair. It will take you some time to figure out how far away they are, and your initial estimate might be too far. God can bring a need into their life that you can meet (or vice versa), and that event will bring you closer together.

Non-Relational Evangelism

Over the last century, many Christians have used proclamational and confrontational forms of evangelism with varying degrees of success: handing out tracts, door-to-door witnessing, evangelistic meetings, radio broadcasts, street or boardwalk campaigns, etc.

The basic idea of such methods is to **throw seed onto soil that God has perfectly conditioned ahead of time.** There are unbelievers out there whose lives have fallen apart, they've come to the end of themselves, and God is convicting them of their spiritual need. There is virtually no distance between your cliff and theirs; having no relationship, you can just reach out with the gospel. A cheerful Christian walks up to them, and – *bing* – the Lord connects the dots, and they respond in faith.

The danger comes in picking unripe fruit. With a single encounter, some believers seem unwilling to wait for the convincing work of the Holy Spirit and press, in salesman-like fashion, for a decision.

The other sad fact is that proclamational and confrontational methods of evangelism have been met with increased resistance due to skepticism about Christianity and fear of cultic groups that use these methods regularly. Also, due to the increased confusion in our culture, sinful people argue that each person must find his or her own "meaning" in some sort of spirituality which is a "private" thing. Talking about religion is like talking about sex – you would never talk about it with a stranger on the street.

DISCUSSION TIME!

How can you start building a relationship with your neighbor if you've lived next door for 10 years and hardly said a word?

Have you ever known a Christian who is really well-liked and respected by his or her unbelieving coworkers? Describe that person.

What might you say to unbelievers who have been "burned" by a Christian neighbor or co-worker?

Starting Redemptive Relationships

We must leave the fortress of the church walls and go into the fields as a farming force—building bridges that span the gulfs of unfamiliarity, and then sowing, watering, and watching God make things grow, person by person, one little patch of land at a time.

Walking and Warring

Sharing your faith is part of your walk with Christ; it involves being guided by the Holy Spirit. He is working right now in the lives of unbelievers you know. He wants you to join Him in the process, but that involves your staying by His side and away from sin, praying for His guidance, and waiting for His promptings moment by moment as you interact with the lost.

Sharing your faith is also an act of war. Satan hates to have lost you, but as long as you stay inactive or in the barracks, you're not a threat. Moving into his territory to rescue other captives is aggressive and hostile to him, and he'll return the favor. Pray for God to protect you and destroy Satan's plots against you.

"And the hand of the Lord was with them, and a great number believed and turned to the Lord."
Acts 11:21

"We know that we are of God, and the whole world lies under the sway of the wicked one."
1 John 5:19

You're Surrounded!

Each of us has a network of relationships. Each day we rub shoulders with all sorts of people – coworkers, store clerks, parents, office staff, salesmen, etc. We need to wake up to the enormous range of possibilities around us! We make contacts through our

DAILY	Location	We live in a neighborhood, we are part of a community, or we have our little niche in cyberspace.
	Vocation	We work at our places of employment or out in the field or on trips.
	Education	We attend school or belong to organizations for further education.
WEEKLY / PERIODICALLY	Acquisition	We go to stores and shops all the time to purchase food, gas, tires, etc.
	Avocation	Our kids are in little league, we are members of a bowling league, the rodeo, or a hobby association, or we work out at the health club.
	Relation	We have family members; some we see frequently, others less frequently.
SUDDENLY	Recreation	We go to the ball park or the county fair or go white-water rafting.
	Situation	We go to the store, our car breaks down along the road, or our health breaks down and we go to the hospital.

"But even if our gospel is veiled, it is veiled to those who are perishing, whose minds the god of this age has blinded, who do not believe, lest the light of the gospel of the glory of Christ, who is the image of God, should shine on them."
2 Corinthians 4:3-4

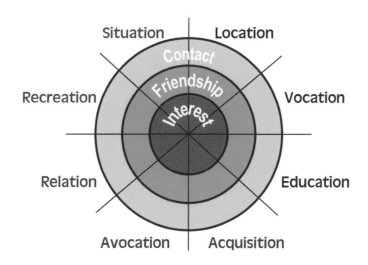

Thinking Redemptively

It has been said that if a believer has been a Christian more than three years, he or she has no unbelieving friends. New believers are often the best at leading others to Christ, yet we often draw them away from their friends. **Mixing it up with unbelievers begins with renewing and disciplining your mind to "think redemptively."** This is a HUGE step in the battle. You have to daily work yourself out of your comfort zone and into the lives of the unbelievers around you.

1. **PRAY AND LOOK FOR OPPORTUNITIES TO MEET THEM** – Ask the Lord to present you with opportunities to mingle with unbelievers. Better still, ask two other believers to pray with you for opportunities, and then report to each other. The Lord can give you opportunities in some very obvious ways – and in some very inconvenient ways (such as your car breaking down). As you pray daily for these opportunities, keep your head up and be ready to spot opportunities when they come.

2. **DISCIPLINE YOURSELF TO INTERACT** – The terrible truth is that sometimes the opportunity comes when you don't want it to, like when you're grumpy, tired at the end of a long day, or frazzled at the end of a business trip. You get out of your car after work, and there is your neighbor raking leaves; what do you do? Smile, nod, and head for the door – or amble over to him and ask how things are going?

3. **LEARN TO ASK QUESTIONS AND LISTEN** – Some of us chatter on when we're nervous. If you're not a people person, you need to have five to ten questions that you are always ready to ask to get or keep the conversation going. One way to "walk in wisdom" is to study the unbelieving people God has put in your life. Listen to your children's friends, and ask questions about their families. Kids seldom hold back.

4. **KEEP A CONTACTS BOOK** – Write down what you learn about your neighbors; it normally helps to write down what you learned as soon as possible, even the same day.

EXERCISE 1: Make a preliminary list below of your contacts. A "contact" is someone who meets the following criteria:
1. **You should know their first name.**
2. **You are able to have contact with them on a regular basis.**
3. **They don't seem to have a personal relationship with Jesus Christ.**

We have left out columns for situation and recreation because often those relationships spring up suddenly and you can't plan them.

Location (Neighbors)	Vocation (Coworkers)	Education (Classmates)	Acquisition (Store Clerks)	Avocation (Fellow Enthusiasts)	Relation (Family members)

> *"Henceforth, we shall be strangers living side by side."*
>
> These words of Juliet were, to her, words of tragedy and despair. For many Christians, it is a way of life with the folks next door!

EXERCISE 2: Before you meet next time, make a little Contacts Book with one page devoted to each person who is a contact of yours. Keep it in a private place, and begin praying for these people each day.

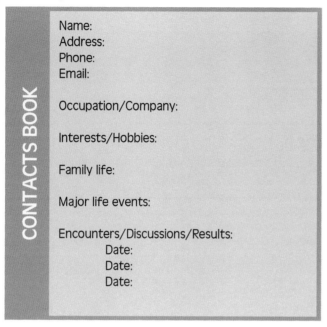

Name:
Address:
Phone:
Email:

Occupation/Company:

Interests/Hobbies:

Family life:

Major life events:

Encounters/Discussions/Results:
    Date:
    Date:
    Date:

Strategic Consumerism

One way to build contacts is through "strategic consumerism" – shopping at the same place on purpose to get to know the employees. The mechanic, the computer store guys, the grocery store check-out clerk, and the video shop attendant are people you can get to know on a first-name basis, if you do it on purpose. Shop during off-peak hours when there are no lines and you can talk a little.

Praying for Them by Name

The Kingdom of God advances on its knees. You have no hope of winning even one person to Christ without God's divine intervention in that person's life. You're asking God to do what you can't – change their hearts and orchestrate opportunities to share Christ.

Pray by name for your unsaved friends, contacts, and neighbors each day. Weeks, even months might go by, and you won't learn too many new facts or have too much interaction, but just keep praying for them by name. As you pass by their home, store, office, or desk, again ask the Lord to do His work in their life.

Time spent walking with God and talking to, learning about, and praying for each of your contacts is crucial in preparing his or her heart to receive the gospel.

THINK LIKE A MISSIONARY

A missionary returning from the field was handed a copy of the Christian Yellow Pages and said:

"So these are all believers? Then these are the places we're NOT supposed to shop . . . there aren't many lost people to win to Christ in these places."

DISCUSSION TIME!

Work through Exercise 1 together. Are you finding that you each have contacts in the same categories (co-workers or neighbors)?

Can any of you share examples of praying for an opportunity to witness, where the Lord answered your prayer very quickly?

What should we be praying for God to do in the steps leading up to someone's salvation?

Buying Up Opportunities

Now you have people that you know by name, and you have started praying for them, asking God to work in their lives. What next?

Remember, You Are Part of a Process

Some sow, others water, but God makes things grow (1 Corinthians 3:5-9). Sowers and reapers will rejoice together (John 4:36). Paul's words give us some comfort. Spiritual life and movement come from God, and we can be part of the process.

> Evangelism is a phase in the process of disciple-making.

Not only are we coworkers with God, we are coworkers with each other. You may never move an unbeliever from a -7 to a +1. Your job may be to move a person up just one step, and another believer will continue the process. Conversely, if you push spiritual truth too far too fast (like pulling on a corn stalk to make it grow), you may actually do more damage than good.

From the chart in Session 5

New Christian	
Seeking forgiveness by faith	-1
Giving in to the gospel and repenting of self-rule	-2
Recognizing a personal problem in relation to God	-3
Wrestling with questions about God, Bible, and the gospel	-4
Grasping the implications of the gospel	-5
Comprehension of the basic gospel	-6
Developing a positive attitude toward the Bible and God	-7
Questioning existing religious concept of God	-8
Has a religious awareness but no knowledge of God	-9
Has no conscious awareness of a Supreme Being	-10

Spiritually Surrendered

Spiritually Interested

Spiritually Disinterested

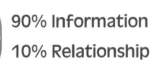

90% Information
10% Relationship

90% Relationship
10% Information

Focus on Relationship or Information?

Once you start talking to an unbelieving neighbor or fellow employee, it doesn't take long to discern whether he or she is spiritually interested or disinterested. **If they are disinterested, you should focus on your relationship** – spend time with them to bring your personal lives together – and sprinkle in truth here and there to create thirst (get them curious). You have to resist the urge to say too much. Trying to cross an unfinished relational bridge may damage your ability to finish the bridge and cross later.

If they are **spiritually interested, you can shift from an emphasis on relationships to a focus on truth**, such as starting a personal or group Bible study. Don't overwhelm them with information! Meet when they want to meet, and let their questions drive your times together. You won't have all the answers. You want to convey that you are a life-long learner about God, Jesus, and the Bible – and they can become a learner too.

> *"For though I am free from all men, I have made myself a servant to all, that I might win the more; and to the Jews I became as a Jew, that I might win the Jews. . . . To the weak I became as the weak that I might win the weak. I have become all things to all men that by all means I might save some. Now I do this for the gospel's sake. . . ."*
> *1 Corinthians 9:19-23*

22 Fostering the Harvest

© 2014 Biblical Ministries Worldwide

Acts of Kindness

"Walk in wisdom toward those on the outside, redeeming the time" (Colossians 4:5). Look for clever, creative ways to buy up opportunities by serving people and meaningfully touching their lives *with no strings attached*. These are the planks on your bridge.

- **When people have little needs, seek to meet them.** Do it in a sincere, nonchalant way, not in a fawning, servile way. Can you pick up the sandwich that they order every day from the deli? If you both need wood chips, could you pick up a few bags for him? Might you care for their dog or bring in their mail when they're on vacation?

- **When people are hurting, help and visit them.** If you see Cindy walking with crutches from her car, something has probably happened in her life. That is the time for you to do something for Cindy . . . make a **meal**, create a **bouquet** with flowers from your garden, or even go out and buy a **card** and write an encouraging note in it. Try to give it to her face to face. Conversation may happen naturally. She is like you. We humans have so much in common. We love to be loved. The Lord loves us immensely, and the most direct way our neighbors can experience His love is through our hands and our voice.

- **Prayer is meaningful to some.** If they have been laid off and are looking for work or someone in their family is sick, you might tell them that you'll pray for them. DON'T FORGET to write it down, pray for the issue, and then follow up later to see how things are going. Tell them you have prayed for them and the situation. People really care about what is near to them – their children, their job, their health, their parents, etc. Write it down, pray it up, and follow it through!

  If they're really facing imminent hardship (like the death of a close relative, or heading back to the front lines in a war), ask them if you can **pray for them right there** where you're standing. Many people truly appreciate that. Some believers even do this in the mall as an evangelistic tool ("prayer evangelism").

- **Let them help you.** Letting people help you might sound strange, but if you always have your act together, you will lack authenticity and transparency. They don't want *your image* as a friend. When they mow your lawn because you're sick, or when they learn your child has a learning disability and give suggestions or share a story, they are drawing closer.

Impersonal Events Away from Home

At first, it is best to get together with neighbors or coworkers **outside your home in an impersonal event**; you may have to plan some, and others just happen. The idea is that you get exposed to each other without becoming too invasive such as a sit down dinner where conversation may be awkward. Look for common ground you have with the person. If you don't have any, try to learn what they're interested in and get involved.

- Go to a ballgame.
- Go to the county fair.
- Go to an auto race (NASCAR).
- Work out at the gym.
- Go hunting or fishing together.
- Go to a cultural event (play, concert, etc.).

Get Them into Your Home

Going inside someone else's house for the first time can be a little intimidating, so **barbeque first** if you can. It's outside; they can see their house or run away if you're really weird or end up trying to sell them something! **Some believers who start home Bible studies find that the neighbors who come have already been in their home for a meal, party, or holiday event.**

Holidays, of course, are a great excuse for having unbelieving friends come over for a party, a meal, or a picnic. Having them bring something sets people more at ease than if you do everything for them. And be careful of making things too perfect. When your dog has puppies, have all the neighbors into your home – not to sell them a puppy, but just to get them inside your home.

Having people in your home is a major step in building a relationship with them. They can see that you are normal. They see that you keep your house clean; they can observe your décor and life. You are bringing your personal lives together.

Reaching Coworkers

Sharing Christ on company time is a real no-no. Before hours or on lunch break is better if that is considered your time. Some are willing to meet for breakfast before work; some may eventually agree to a Bible study at lunch break. The ideal arrangement is to bring your personal worlds together because the gospel is a personal issue.

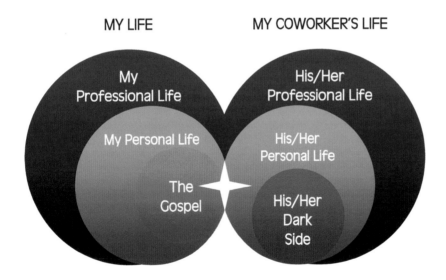

MY LIFE   MY COWORKER'S LIFE

My Professional Life — His/Her Professional Life
My Personal Life — His/Her Personal Life
The Gospel — His/Her Dark Side

DISCUSSION TIME!

Have you ever had someone from work join your family for a social event away from home?

Ever had them join you for dinner? How did the conversation go?

List 10 questions you should have ready at any time to keep the conversation moving.

List several activities that you and the unbelievers around you would enjoy.

Watering and Harvesting

Seed, Soil, and Germination

Building bridges of loving and trusting friendship into the lives of unbelievers takes time. Once you cross the bridge and sow the seed of the gospel in their lives, you again need to be patient. Seed has a germination time. The seed needs water and warmth and good soil; then it dies and splits with new life from the inside.

Every piece of ground is different. In Matthew 13, Jesus spoke about four types of soil:

- The hard soil lets the seed stay on top until birds carried it away (a **hard heart** that needs some tilling).
- The second bit of soil was sparse. The seed sprung up and withered without fruit (a **shallow heart** that likes Christian people and ideas but never commits to Christ).
- The third plot of soil gave root to the seed but thorns choked out all growth (a **distracted heart** that agrees to Christian truth but is more focused on family, work, and wealth).
- The fourth plot of soil was tilled, receptive, and not riddled with weeds (a **tender heart** that receives the seed and produces life that bears fruit).

Like the crowd that heard Paul's address at Mars Hill, some mocked, some said they wanted to hear more, and some believed (Acts 17:32-24). Our job is to scatter good seed.

> *"I planted, Apollos watered, but God gave the increase. So then neither he who plants is anything, nor he who waters, but God who gives the increase. Now he who plants and he who waters are one, and each one will receive his own reward according to his own labor."*
> *1 Corinthians 3:6-8*

Transitioning Conversations

You can build relationships and build an unbeliever's spiritual curiosity at the same time through **helpful** (grace = help) and **thirst-provoking** conversation.

> *Let your speech always be with grace, seasoned with salt, that you may know how you ought to answer each one.*
> *Colossians 4:6*

Gracious conversation is kind and others-oriented. Your neighbor may not deserve it – we don't deserve it! Some Christians always turn the conversation back to themselves – not good. What is your neighbor interested in? What do your coworkers talk about? In a conversation, you should try to move the topic from surface to meaningful to spiritual to gospel.

1. START WITH A RELATIONAL ISSUE, something in which you have a common interest – soccer, racing cars, storms, golf, boats, politics, children, drought, etc. Ask lots of questions. People love to talk about themselves and their opinions!
2. LOOK TO MOVE THE CONVERSATION TO MORE MEANINGFUL ASPECTS of the topic as time goes on (why I rear my kids the way I do, the fear and despair people face with terrorism or social upheaval, etc.). I continue to ask for their opinions. By giving them a chance to air their opinions, you earn the right to voice some of yours down the line.
3. TRANSITION THE CONVERSATION FROM MEANINGFUL TO SPIRITUAL. You can talk about what's important in life, life after death, people with wrong priorities, handling suffering, the problem of evil in the world. Try asking some of their questions like, "Do you think it's intellectually responsible to believe in God?" You can eventually ask, "Where are you in your spiritual journey?"
4. MOVE FROM SPIRITUAL TO THE GOSPEL. "Do you think a person can really know if he is going to heaven when he dies?" If you were to die and God asked you, 'Why should I let you into heaven?' what would you say?"

The speed of transitioning conversations depends upon the person with whom you are dealing. Jesus moved quite quickly with the woman at the well in John 4.

Relational
↓
Meaningful
↓
Spiritual
↓
Gospel

Sprinkling Salt

In our haste to give people the water of the gospel, we fail to consider if they are really thirsty. Colossians 4:6 says our conversations should be "sprinkled with salt." It is a real art form to try and create spiritual thirst in the person to whom you are speaking. You want them to ask something like, "What is the gospel?" or "How does a person become a Christian?"

You create thirst by sprinkling salt in your conversation, nonchalantly mentioning activities of a God-centered life (praying, viewing our kids as gifts from the Lord, being thankful about knowing where we would have gone had we been in that auto accident). At times you'll see thirst, such as when you are in a meaningful conversation and they transition the topic to God, Jesus, the Bible, etc.

Giving Them Time

Remember that evangelism is a phase of discipleship; it is a process. As you sow the Truth into the minds of your unbelieving friends, you must allow time for things to sink in. There is little that you can do to enhance the germination process. For a seed to spring to life, conditions must be right, conditions that the Lord controls. Waiting flies in the face of our "more, better, faster" culture, but we are to follow God's lead, not force His hand.

At no time in anyone's life does Bible knowledge necessarily equal a changed heart or life. Dr. Paul Benjamin conducted hundreds of interviews with new believers, and in his book, *The Equipping Ministry*, he wrote that the average person requires five "significant encounters" with the gospel (hearing it clearly so that it registers with the heart) before accepting Christ.

Meeting for Serious Study

Sometimes unbelievers are interested in doing a study of Christian ideas.
- You can design your own Bible study, preferably in Genesis or John. The Journey Studies at Oak Village are provided with this material as an example of what you might do in a neighborhood Bible study.
- Use the Creation-To-Christ approach of the Firm Foundations materials published by New Tribes Mission.
- Use The Stranger on the Road to Emmaus book and study guide by John Cross.
- Use a basic Bible concepts course with sufficient content for an unbeliever to feel conviction of sin and make an intelligent commitment to Jesus Christ.

This Bible study is based on your relationship, so avoid moving it to a formal setting. Meet in a restaurant or in your home. Keep it relaxed and informal, and don't let meetings go too long unless they insist. Consider making it four to six weeks long, and see if they have further interest from that point (leaving it open-ended gives them no easy way out). Let them drive the process. They may even invite friends.

If you're studying the Bible, stay with the text rather than teaching something they can't see in front of them. If you're preparing your own material, spend a significant amount of preparation time adapting your material to an unbeliever's level of understanding. We often use Christian terms and concepts with which they are totally unfamiliar.

With prayer, time, relationships, gracious and salt-sprinkled conversations, and the Lord's work in churning their heart with conviction, unbelievers normally make the conversational move to ask about praying to God or getting baptized, or starting to go to church. Don't tell them where they are spiritually; ask them. At times, they will commit their lives to Christ without telling you. The seed has come to life.

See Appendix E for the story of the Oak Village Bible study that took place several years ago near Atlanta.

Giving Value to Opinions

Give value to the opinions of your unbelieving friends at all times. You draw people out by asking for their opinions. Giggling or blurting out a laugh when they talk about aliens, missing books of the Bible, or God being a transcendent force will set you way back. An embarrassed or belittled person will not open up again very soon.

Witnessing is not "winning" an argument so that the unbeliever gives in. One of the major barriers to interpersonal communication lies in our natural tendency to judge – to hastily approve or disapprove – the statements of another person. Replying with statements like "You're not serious that. . . ." or "It's a proven fact that. . . ." can be damaging.

They may bring up divisive topics, but you shouldn't. Stand your ground only on the critical hills. If they believe in God but also mention that they believe in evolution, don't try to set them straight on evolution first; keep moving toward their heart's relationship with God. Also avoid attacking religious associations or denominations. Avoid stating that they could not be Christians. Identification with a church organization does not affect one's salvation, and discussing differences can lead to unnecessary hostility.

Some opinions are right, some are wrong, but all are valuable.

Uh, that's grace seasoned with salt, not salt seasoned with grace!

DISCUSSION TIME!

We could not possibly write out "canned" ways to transition all of the conversations you might have, but do some role play. Pair up, take a topic or two, begin talking and have one person try to move the conversation to a meaningful or spiritual level.

What are some things you could say to create spiritual thirst in a person?

Do you think that you could teach a basic Bible study in your home?

Are your relationships with several unbelievers to the point where you could ask if they would be interested in a brief set of Bible studies?

Closing Thoughts

Biblically Anchored; Culturally Flexible

In the old days, an Arapaho chief facing battle would stake himself to a spot of ground so as not to run or give ground in battle. He would tie his leg to a 4- to 6-foot tether that was tied to the stake. He wouldn't yield his position, but he could move freely about the stake depending on the direction of the attack.

This is how we should view the gospel. The gospel message is changeless and transcends time and culture. But while God's truth never changes, our culture and society do change. How does this affect evangelism and discipleship? How do we bring unchanging truth to a changing world?

There are different angles, emphases, or themes a Christian can take in communicating God's truth. For instance, in presenting the gospel, you could
- Emphasize the **judicial aspects** of the gospel (a sinner condemned by a holy judge who can then be declared righteous), or
- Emphasize the **relational aspects** of the gospel (a hostile child of Satan, adopted by God and restored to loving acceptance), or
- Emphasize the **proprietary aspects** of the gospel (a person taken captive by the enemy and lost in the slave market of sin but redeemed by a benevolent Creator), or
- Emphasize the **sacrificial aspects** of the gospel (a person alone in darkness with no way back to God, but Jesus selflessly sacrificed Himself for us to open the way back to God.

Different aspects of the Lord's multi-faceted gospel seem to "connect" with certain personalities and certain generations. Several authors have commented that the relational and sacrificial aspects of the gospel seem to connect with the younger generations.

Healthier for Everyone

Personal evangelism benefits the disciple. D. Martyn Lloyd-Jones noted that the thrust of a Christian's spiritual life seems to be determined by the thrust of their conversion experience. One who is cajoled into the kingdom with little information will have to be cajoled throughout their Christian life and be content with little information. One who is led to Christ through a personal relationship will also find it natural to be discipled to strength in Christ by a mentor. Therefore, personal and relational evangelism sets the pattern for the healthiest path of spiritual growth.

Personal evangelism also benefits you. Ask anyone who has done it. There are few joys like seeing the Lord turn the lights on in a person's heart where you are guiding but not pushing the process. It is like watching a fetal monitor everyday as a little one is formed in the womb. 1 Corinthians 3:9 says that we are co-workers together with God, and discipling someone to Christ is one of those times when you really *feel* that you and God are working together as a team. Wow! What a privilege!

> "Brethren, if anyone among you wanders from the truth, and someone turns him back, let him know that he who turns a sinner from the error of his way will save a soul from death, and cover a multitude of sins."
> James 5:19-20

Most of all, sharing your faith benefits the Lord. You obviously consider Him worthy if you're willing to get out of your comfort zone and risk rejection by telling others about Him and what He has done for us. If He blesses you with the opportunity to lead someone to saving faith, you have helped to create one more worshipper of Jesus Christ. To Him be the glory!

Appendix A – Evangelistic Styles

Examining Evangelistic Styles

In the modern church, roughly six common approaches have been used by Christians to present the gospel to others. The New Testament contains examples of each method. Review the description and dangers of each.

INSTITUTIONAL STYLES

	DESCRIPTION	THE DANGERS ARE...
PROCLAMATIONAL *Acts 2:14-39* *Acts 17:22-31*	Giving a public statement of the truth of the gospel in the church or in public	Failing to give an opportunity for dialogue, and seeming a little eccentric in many cultures
INVITATIONAL *John 1:41-42*	Inviting someone to a Bible study or church service where the gospel is presented	Never sharing the gospel yourself - a person who can't articulate their own salvation experience lacks credibility

The two styles in blue are the leading traditional methods used by churches and believers in those assemblies. They reflect an approach where most believers do not share the faith but bring the lost to those who can.

INDIVIDUAL STYLES

	DESCRIPTION	THE DANGERS ARE...
INTELLECTUAL *Acts 17:17* *Acts 19:8*	Advocating the reasonableness of the Christian faith through apologetics, creationism, and philosophy	Losing focus on the gospel, forgetting love and relationships, and becoming contentious
TESTIMONIAL *John 9:25* *Acts 26:1-23*	Sharing with a person the difference Christ has made in your life – purpose, joy, meaning, hope – and urging others to find the same	Being so "experiential" in your explanation that you do not clearly cover all elements of the gospel
CONVERSATIONAL *John 3:1-21, 4:5-26*	Presenting the gospel to a person as the result of a transitioned conversation while handling questions and objections	Being more incidental than purposeful, failing to create thirst in the listener, presenting the gospel in too many pieces, and not "putting the puzzle together"
CONFRONTATIONAL *Acts 26:27-29*	Presenting a simple gospel to a person while skirting side issues and objections in order to press for a decision	Picking unripe fruit, giving an incomplete gospel, obtaining false decisions and giving false assurances

The four styles in green reflect a more individualized approach where believers who have been equipped are able to share their faith one-on-one with unbelievers. Some believers choose to dialogue and handle questions; others simply share how God has transformed their life; other Christians try to move into the gospel in everyday conversations; still other believers engage in evangelism as a truth encounter with little or no need for a relationship.

> All six evangelistic styles can and have been used effectively.
> All are biblical, and all are legitimate forms of evangelism.

Bridge-Building Non-Evangelism

Many believers prefer to simply live a good and different life in front of their neighbors and coworkers, and invite them to church so that they can hear the gospel presented by their pastor or a special speaker. In many churches, this is encouraged by pastors who include the gospel in virtually every message.

BRIDGE-BUILDING STYLES

	DESCRIPTION	THE DANGERS ARE. . .
LIFESTYLE *Matthew 5:13-16*	Being a silent witness of a transformed life that will lead others to wonder what makes the difference.	Not saying anything. The spoken word must be eventually added to the living testimony. The Great Commission is to make disciples, not just "live."
RELATIONAL *Matthew 9:9-13* *1 Corinthians 9:16-23*	Building bridges of loving and trusting friendships into people's lives (redemptive relationships) to disciple a person to Christ.	Taking too long to build the bridge (being incidental rather than purposeful).
CHARITABLE *Romans 13:8-12*	Serving individuals in the community with acts of kindness (providing food, clothing, relief, services, etc.)	Not saying anything or portraying the gospel as merely alleviating human suffering, something known as "the social gospel."

While charitable deeds and living transformed lives are an excellent foundation for sharing the gospel later, many believers view these things as synonymous with evangelism. They are not.

Appendix B - The Security of the Believer

If we are truly saved, we can never lose our salvation!

- John 1:12-13 – When you receive God's free gift, God makes you His ADOPTED CHILD.
- John 10:28-29 – God gives us ETERNAL life that no one can take away.
- John 6:37-40 – Those who come to Christ He will not CAST OUT.
- 1 John 5:12-13 – We can KNOW that we are eternally saved.
- 1 John 1:9 – Regularly CONFESS your sins to God, and He will FORGIVE and CLEANSE you.

Appendix C – Apologetics Resources

By "apologetics" we don't mean apologizing. By "arguments" we don't mean arguing! The English word "apologetics" comes from the Greek word meaning to defend, to make a reply, or to give an answer as in a courtroom defense. An argument is a line of reasoning in defense of your position.

Peter admonished Christians to be ready to give a reason for the hope we have (1 Peter 3:15). Apologetics is, therefore, a whole system of arguments in defense of the Divine origin and authority of the Christian faith.

1. **Primary Apologetic Issues**
   Arguments supporting the existence of God
   - **Cosmological** – there must be a first cause in the creation that/who is uncaused, and there must be a sustaining force.
   - **Teleological** – the design of creation and of man indicates an intelligent, creative designer.
   - **Ontological** – man has an incurable belief that there is a greater being (the God-shaped void in the heart).
   - **Moral/Rational** – basic morals and truth transcend time and culture and are not evolutionary. Thus, moral laws are given by a non-human lawgiver.

   Arguments supporting the Bible as God's only special revelation
   - **Internal Evidences** – Prophecies with 100% accuracy, accurate in history and science, overall theme unlikely devised by man (man is utterly sinful and unable to save himself), lack of hero-worship, claims divine authorship, salvation by faith rather than works, cohesive message despite 40+ authors over 1600 years, etc.
   - **External Evidences** – Extent of translation, worldwide impact, survival through persecution, ability to change lives and cultures, etc.

   Arguments supporting the fact that Jesus is God in human flesh
   - Claimed to be equal with God
   - Bible passages claim His identity as God
   - His miracles over nature, disease, and death
   - Undeniable facts surrounding His resurrection

2. **Secondary Apologetic Issues (Handling Critics)**
   You should also make it a point to learn some facts and arguments in the creation v. evolution debate. Evolution is the single greatest set of ideas to challenge the Christian faith in Church history.
   - How can I believe the Bible when it denies evolution?
   - How can an all-powerful and all-loving God exist if there is evil and suffering in the world?
   - Is hell really eternal fire?
   - Is Jesus the only way?
   - What about those who have never heard?
   - What about the devout of other religions?
   - Is man controlled or free?
   - What about the "mistakes" in the Bible?

Good Apologetics Books

For Your Unbelieving Friends:
Ultimate Questions, John Blanchard, Evangelical Press, 1992
The Case for Faith, Lee Strobel, Zondervan Corp., 2000
The Case for Christ, Lee Strobel, Zondervan Corp., 1998
The New Evidence That Demands a Verdict, Josh McDowell, Thomas Nelson, 1999
Does God Believe in Atheists? John Blanchard, Evangelical Press
Meet the Real Jesus, John Blanchard, Evangelical Press, 2000
Jesus Among Other Gods, Ravi Zacharias, Thomas Nelson, 2002
Can Man Live Without God? Ravi Zacharias, Thomas Nelson, 1996
The Lotus and the Cross: Jesus Talks with Buddha, Ravi Zacharias, Multnomah Publ., 2001

For Your Education and Improvement:
A Ready Defense, Josh McDowell, Thomas Nelson, 1993
When Critics Ask, Norman Geisler, Baker, 1992
When Skeptics Ask, Norman Geisler, Baker, 1990
Encyclopedia of Christian Apologetics, Geisler, editor, Baker, 1999
Classical Apologetics, R.C. Sproul, Zondervan Corp., 1984
Boyd's Handbook of Practical Apologetics, Robert Boyd, Kregel Publications, 1996
Apologetics to the Glory of God, John M. Frame, Presbyterian & Reformed, 1994

Appendix D – Christian Decision-Making

As believers, we desire to please the Lord fully through holiness and devotion to His will. But godly people will differ on personal conduct (music, education, dress, dancing, etc.) based on their understanding of the Scriptures. Here is a suggested framework for making God-honoring decisions on these issues.

Specific Commands

WHAT THESE ARE: These are all of the commands of Scripture that are crystal clear in their prohibitions.

Examples of specific commands:

Do not steal	Do not commit adultery
Do not murder	Do not commit perjury

WHAT TO DO: Don't even ask the Holy Spirit for guidance since the Spirit never leads contrary to the Word of God. Pray for the Lord to give you the resolve and strength to obey Him.

If the Scripture says nothing "on point" about the action, go to the next level
↓ ↓ ↓ ↓ ↓

General Commands and Historical Illustrations

WHAT THESE ARE: These are commands found in the Scriptures that are subject to varying applications due to the words used, and the stories of the Bible that illustrate poor choices.

Examples of general commands:	*Examples of historical illustrations:*
Flee youthful lusts	Joseph fleeing Potiphar's wife
Be not drunk with wine	Noah getting drunk in his tent

WHAT TO DO: Study the Scriptures thoroughly, and pray for the Holy Spirit to give you wisdom and guide your study in coming to your personal position on the issue. Then ask the Lord for the resolve and strength to follow your decisions. Also, give other believers the latitude to come to somewhat differing conclusions than yours.

If the Scripture still does not prohibit the action, heed biblical cautions and go to the next level
↓ ↓ ↓ ↓ ↓

Christian Liberty

WHAT THIS IS: If you conclude, after study, that the Bible does not prohibit the action, you have biblical "liberty" to do it.

WHAT TO DO: You must still pay attention to a few more Scriptural limitations. Pray and ask the Lord to help you act with a careful consciousness of others and your own purity and testimony.

A	**Appearances** – Avoid the appearance (all kinds) of evil as judged by the common man.	1 Thessalonians 5:22
B	**Brotherhood** – Don't exercise your liberty and cause another believer who doesn't feel he has that liberty to violate his conscience and sin.	Romans 14:13-15, 21; 1 Corinthians 8:9-13; 10:23-29
C	**Conscience** – Don't violate your own conscience in doing something you are hesitant about in your spirit.	Romans 14:22-23
D	**Deception** – Don't cloak your stubborn sinfulness by claiming that you have liberty.	1 Peter 2:16
E	**Eldership** – Don't disobey the instructions of authorities who may choose to limit your conduct more than the Scriptures do (parents, church leaders, school authorities).	Hebrews 13:7,17

Appendix E – Neighborhood Bible Studies

Watching the Lights Come On
By David J. Brown, Biblical Ministries Worldwide

SUBDIVISION MISSION FIELD
Oak Village is a quiet little subdivision that was carved out of the woods northeast of Atlanta about 15 years ago. Trees that echo the voices of squealing children flank its winding lanes. It's a nice place to live. Karin and I and our four children moved to Oak Village many months ago fearing that we would be surrounded by Baptists. We like Baptists, we are Baptists, but we were looking for people who didn't think they were believers.

We hit the jackpot! Our new neighbors came over and introduced themselves in the fine Southern tradition, and we discovered that most of them were unchurched folks from Baptist, Methodist, and Catholic backgrounds. We began praying for them by name each day. After all, it is God who softens hearts and opens blind eyes and deaf ears.

DOING THINGS TOGETHER
We developed good relationships with them in the first year. We watched their pets, brought in their mail, and watered their plants when they were gone. Our kids played together. Our property, located at the corner of two cul-de-sacs, became the neighborhood rallying point for kids on bikes, skateboards, and scooters. We got a dog that kids love – a Cocker Spaniel. We showed love to their kids. We raked leaves together, exchanged stories, and laughed. When they wanted to help us with the lawn or the deck, we let them. On occasion, we even asked them for their help and then returned the favor later. We shared fireworks on July 4th, and cookies at Christmas.

If the conversation turned to meaningful things, we would try to transition to spiritual things – that our kids were blessings from the Lord, for instance. They would agree and then start spilling their take on God, religion, church, etc. We have learned that many people have a real spiritual interest but don't like "church" – the big group, the impersonal atmosphere, the money grab, and of course, the hypocritical people; we heard all of the typical complaints unbelievers have about churches.

GOALS FOR OUR NEIGHBORS
Our ultimate goal was to present these dear friends to the Lord as those who want to worship Him in Spirit and in truth and serve Him as equipped servant-leaders. Our mid-range goal was to see them come to Christ. Our short-range goal was to have a non-threatening, "explorers" Bible study with them. We didn't think that they would ever come into a strange house to study the Bible. But they might come into a warm and familiar house to do so.

Therefore, one of the most important things we did in evangelizing our lost neighbors was to invite them for tea, for a cookout, or for dinner. Karin would be talking with one of the ladies by the curb and invite her in for tea. Well, this was just ta-ta for American ladies who normally drink instant coffee from a mug. Karin had the lace doilies, and the china tea service. She served it just like we did in South Africa – sugar in the cup, then milk, then tea. And then they would chat. A couple months later we would have the family over for dinner and games. They had known our kids, our dog, our phone number, and us. But now they knew our house.

A HOME BIBLE STUDY

After 14 months of building relationships, we floated the idea of a neighborhood family Bible study with our neighbor, April. She said she would love to have one, and she felt several others would be interested as well! April invited most of our neighbors (the most evangelistic unbeliever we ever saw), and we invited a few others. The response was overwhelming!

We began the study in September, when the "back-to-school spirit" was in the air. The whole family was invited. My sons, Joshua and Nicolas (ages 15 and 11 respectively), were given charge of the 3- to 12-year-olds upstairs in the boys' room. They watched a Bible video, had the kids color a paper dealing with the same story, and then had each child use Legos to build a scene from the video. My daughter Stephanie (age 14) took care of the babies upstairs in her room. Families showed up at 7, got the kids settled in, got tea or coffee and we began by 7:15. I told Josh to let the kids go at 8 to keep me from rambling and to get the kids to bed on time. We usually had tea and pastry, and then everyone headed home.

SIMPLE HANDOUT

I developed one-page handouts for each study. I began the first study with some core values:

- This Bible study is a tool, not a tradition, and we can end it whenever we want to.
- Come casual, and come with the kids.
- Most Bible learning in church is one-way lecture. We want to try and answer questions and talk about issues.
- Everyone's opinion is important and worth considering.
- We will study the Bible just like we read letters – in a literal, grammatical, and historical way, unless the context clearly indicates otherwise.

Then I began, "This is a Bible. It has two divisions. Does anyone know what they are?" It was just that basic. Then I reviewed facts about the Bible and where it came from. April went home, called a relative in Indiana and read her the entire handout! A while later, we received a card from that friend telling us that we were the answer to 20 years of prayer that she had lifted to the Lord for April and her family.

WHAT A GROUP!

We had an interesting mix of people from different theological grids, and we found tremendous joy in teaching the Bible to adults who had never heard the stories before! They interacted with each other, had lots of questions, and at times gave the most hysterical answers! Some were right on the money; others were out there in left field and involved aliens, karma, and shivers.

I started in the Book of Genesis. The power of God, the creation, the fall of Satan, responsibility and fall of mankind, and the beginning of self-made religion are all in the first four chapters. Lisa is one of our committed learners. She is a Jewish friend who rescued our family when our car broke down on northbound Interstate 85 – just before the Bible study began. Genesis 3:22 says, "Behold, man has become like one of us, knowing good and evil." Lisa interrupts, "Like one of *us*? Who is *us*? Who else is God speaking to?" I responded that although God is one, there are also these strange little hints in Genesis that God is a plurality. Lisa was thinking.

Lisa often stayed afterward until midnight. She kept asking questions and once thanked us for giving her time to think through things. She has a very high view of God. She can't see how Jesus could be God. I challenged her as to whether God could be in heaven and on earth at the same time. I showed her the bodily appearances of God in the Old Testament ... a light went on. I read her the last part of Isaiah 52 and all of 53. She thought it was from one of the gospels. I turned my Bible around and showed her that it was from HER scriptures. Another light went on. She got chills. "Oooh, it must be the Holy Spirit!" she said, and we laughed.

EXPLAIN THE GOSPEL TO ME!

Some of the others noticed Lisa staying and wondered if they could stay and ask questions. April said, "I have to admit, I always thought the gospel was just the whole Bible, so I'm a bit confused. Could you explain really slowly what the gospel is exactly?" We had already discussed the concept of sacrificial lambs when we talked about Cain and Abel – how God allowed our death penalty to be transferred to a substitute. I used a Strong's Concordance as the record book of our sins and covered it with our sheepskin. The book was still there, just covered. "That's atonement," I said. Then, after explaining the need for a human substitute to fully remove the sin, I threw the sheepskin over the concordance, but slipped the concordance out of sight. Lisa interjected, "So with Jesus, the sin isn't covered - it's gone." More lights went on. Two hours later they went home with a lot to think about.

CAN WE GET BAPTIZED?

When you present the gospel in this non-confrontational way and don't press for a decision, be sure to listen for them to begin talking about baptism. In January April asked if I could baptize their 10-year-old son, Zachary, since I was "a reverend, and all that." I said "yeeaaah." Then April said that she was thinking of getting baptized too. "Okaaayyy," I said. Then Larry said, "Well, we just need to nail down where we are with God. Could you come over for dinner?" That Sunday afternoon, as we all cried, both Larry and April committed their lives to Christ.

In March, the doctors discovered that Andy had cancer. When his young bride had been killed at age 22, Andy had walked away from God for 25 years. The Lord had opened his heart at our Bible study, but Andy said he needed a mule kick to make him commit his life to Christ. Cancer was the kick, and he and his wife Jane, a former Roman Catholic, trusted Christ.

We finished the Book of Genesis in 31 studies by the end of July. During those ten months we had an average of 10 adults and 8 kids per week. Many expressed that the study was the highlight of their week. We have been thrilled to see our neighbors come to know Christ simply by studying the Book of Genesis.

THIS IS DISCIPLESHIP

My wife and I believe that discipleship is life-change toward Christlikeness in the context of relationships. Discipleship can begin while our friends are still unbelievers. It prepares them to make an intelligent commitment to Christ; and once they are in Christ, the pattern for Christian growth has already been established. Discipleship is easy for us to understand because Jesus modeled it for us. Discipleship is hard to do because it doesn't mesh with our institutional church culture, and we are often too busy to spend "that kind of time" with a person.

Repeatedly presenting God's Word in an atmosphere of trust and friendship enhances the "ripening process." We have seldom had so much fun, not just because we're teaching the Bible, but because in mentoring our unbelieving neighbors, we're having the privilege of watching the lights come on.

ABOUT THE AUTHOR

David J. Brown, JD, PhD, is a Philadelphia lawyer who prepared for ministry in his local church and then made the jump "from law to grace" in 1995, joining the church-planting team of Biblical Ministries Worldwide in Johannesburg, South Africa. Since then, David has served as a church-planter and pastor in three church-planting projects, and has started a ministry to AIDS orphans. David is also a professor of theology and ethics in South Africa and has served both as the mission's Area Director for Europe and Area Director for Africa.

Made in the USA
Charleston, SC
27 November 2014